Morse Code Quilts

Material Messages for Loved Ones

Sarah J. Maxwell

Morse Code Quilts
by Sarah J. Maxwell

Landauer Publishing *(www.landauerpub.com)* is an imprint of
Fox Chapel Publishing Company, Inc.

Project Team:
Vice President-Content: Christopher Reggio
Editors: Laurel Albright/Sue Voegtlin
Copy Editor: Anthony Regolino
Designer: Laurel Albright
Photographer: Sue Voegtlin

ISBN: 978-1-947163-06-5

Library of Congress Cataloging-in-Publication Data

Names: Maxwell, Sarah (Sarah J.), author.
Title: Morse code quilts / Sarah Maxwell.
Description: Mount Joy, PA : Landauer Publishing, [2019]
Identifiers: LCCN 2019003115 | ISBN 9781947163065 (pbk.)
Subjects: LCSH: Patchwork quits. | Patchwork--Patterns. | Quilting--Patterns.
| Morse code--Miscelanea.
Classification: LCC TT835 .M2736958 2019 | DDC 746.46/041--dc23
LC record available at https://lccn.loc.gov/2019003115

We are always looking for talented authors. To submit an idea, please send a brief inquiry to
acquisitions@foxchapelpublishing.com.

Printed in Singapore

21 20 19   2 4 6 8 10 9 7 5 3 1

Contents

–·–·/––––/–·/–·/·/–·/–/···/

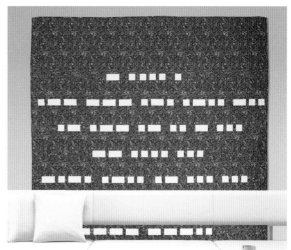

The World Awaits   14

Message in the Dark   20

Peace 36

Snow 48

Love You More 26

Merry 40

Across the Myles 52

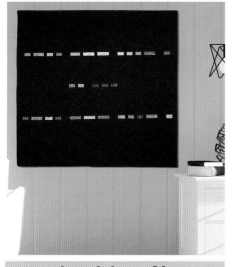

Love Is Love 30

Hugs 44

The Adventure Begins 58

Introduction

About Morse Code

Morse code was created in the early 1800s as a method of transmitting information across telegraph wires. Long before the days of the U.S. Postal Service, fax machines, email, and social media, individuals and government leaders needed a fast, reliable way to exchange information across great distances.

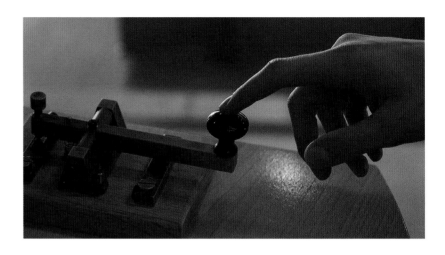

As scientists discovered that electrical current could be stored in battery form and that electrical current could be disrupted with magnets, they began experimenting with how that knowledge could be used to create a communication system. Researchers on both sides of the Atlantic are credited with important contributions to the creation of the telegraph system and the resulting code that allowed for communication. Americans Samuel Morse and Alfred Vail developed a code based on a series of dots (short pulses) and dashes (longer pulses) that telegraph operators memorized so they could quickly transcribe letters as the communication was received.

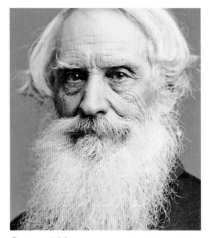

Samuel Morse

Alfred Vail

Decoding the Code

Morse code is a series of dots and dashes that represent each letter of the alphabet and each number. When converting Morse code to a "quilt code," the dots, dashes, spaces between units within a letter, and space between words, all contribute to the size of a word or phrase. The following illustration shows how each unit is counted. At this point, you will be calculating units, not measurements. (Actual Morse code for communication has slightly different spacing requirements than what I use for fabric messages. My conventions prevent the design from becoming an unmanageable width.)

The dot is 1 unit.

A dash is 2 units, or two times the dot measurement.

The space between parts in a letter is half a unit.

The spaces between letters in a word is one and a half units The illustration below is the word "sew."

The space between words in a single row is equal to 3 units. The illustration below spells out "sew it."

When I design a quilt, I start by choosing my phrase. I write out the words on paper and determine how many units of space each word requires. For example, the word "Love" looks like the illustration below, in Morse code. The charts I've provided on pages 9–13 give you the unit counts for numbers, letters, and months.

L=6.5 units   O=7 units   V=6.5 units   E=1 unit

Next, you'll add the letter spacers, (3) 1.5 units, and that brings the unit count to 25.5 units. Below, the word "Love" is illustrated in "quilt code" dot/dash units.

L=6.5 units | 1.5 units | O=7 units | 1.5 units | V=6.5 units | 1.5 units | E=1 unit

Now a measurement has to be assigned to the unit.

Once I have my unit count, I decide how big I want my quilt to be. For instance, the Love You More quilt, on page 26, finishes at 42" by 50". I need to assign sizes to the phrase units to work within the width of 42". You may have to experiment with several unit measurements to see what fills the width of your quilt. Remember that the longest word will probably determine the width of your quilt.

If I used 1" for finished dot size, then 25.5 units times 1" equals 25½". This is not enough to fill the 42" width of my quilt.

If I used 2" for a finished unit size, then 25.5 units times 2" equals 51". This is too big for the width.

Using 1½" for my finished unit size worked perfectly with a little room to add fabric at the ends of the rows. 25.5 units times 1½" equals 38½".

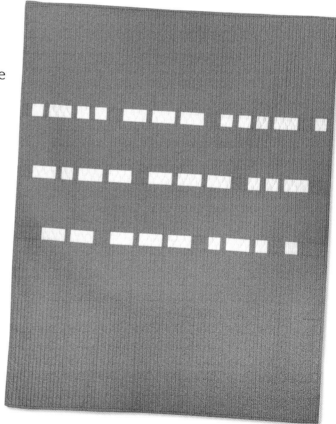

Morse Code Number Chart

Morse Code	Quilt Code	Unit Count
1 ● ▬ ▬ ▬ ▬	▮▯▮▯▮	11
2 ● ● ▬ ▬ ▬	▮▯▮▮▯▮	10
3 ● ● ● ▬ ▬	▮▮▮▯▮	9
4 ● ● ● ● ▬	▮▮▮▮▯▮	8
5 ● ● ● ● ●	▮▮▮▮▮	7
6 ▬ ● ● ● ●	▮▯▮▮▮▮	8
7 ▬ ▬ ● ● ●	▮▯▮▯▮▮▮	9
8 ▬ ▬ ▬ ● ●	▮▯▮▯▮▯▮	10
9 ▬ ▬ ▬ ▬ ●	▮▯▮▯▮▯▮	11
0 ▬ ▬ ▬ ▬ ▬	▮▯▮▯▮▯▮	12

Morse Code Letter Chart A–M

	Morse Code	Quilt Code	Unit Count
A	● ▬		3.5
B	▬ ● ● ●		6.5
C	▬ ● ▬ ●		7.5
D	▬ ● ●		5
E	●		1
F	● ● ▬ ●		6.5
G	▬ ▬ ●		6
H	● ● ● ●		5.5
I	● ●		2.5
J	● ▬ ▬ ▬		8.5
K	▬ ● ▬		6
L	● ▬ ● ●		6.5
M	▬ ▬		4.5

Morse Code Letter Chart N–Z

	Morse Code	Quilt Code	Unit Count
N	▬ ●		3.5
O	▬ ▬ ▬		7
P	● ▬ ▬ ●		7.5
Q	▬ ▬ ● ▬		8.5
R	● ▬ ●		5
S	● ● ●		4
T	▬		2
U	● ● ▬		5
V	● ● ● ▬		6.5
W	● ▬ ▬		6
X	▬ ● ● ▬		7.5
Y	▬ ● ▬ ▬		8.5
Z	▬ ▬ ● ●		7.5

Morse Code Month Charts

I've translated each month into code for easy reference if you need a month spelled out. The count starts with the first unit and ends with the last. If a month is followed by another name, or year, the unit space will equal three times the dot unit measurement. Remember, this is only a unit count. Apply your dot/dash/spacers, referring to page 7.

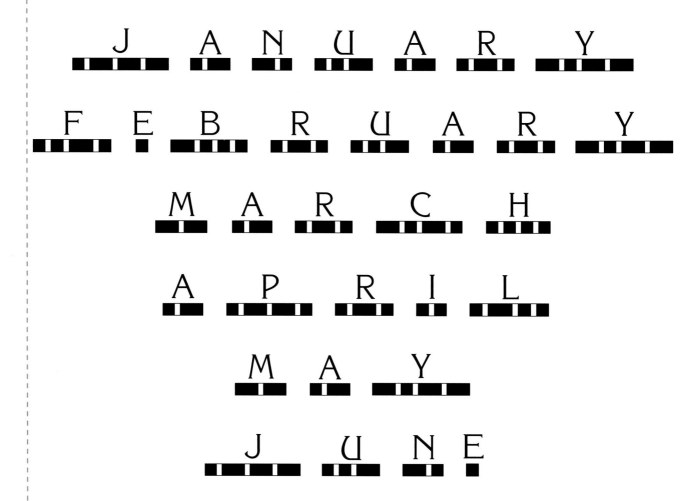

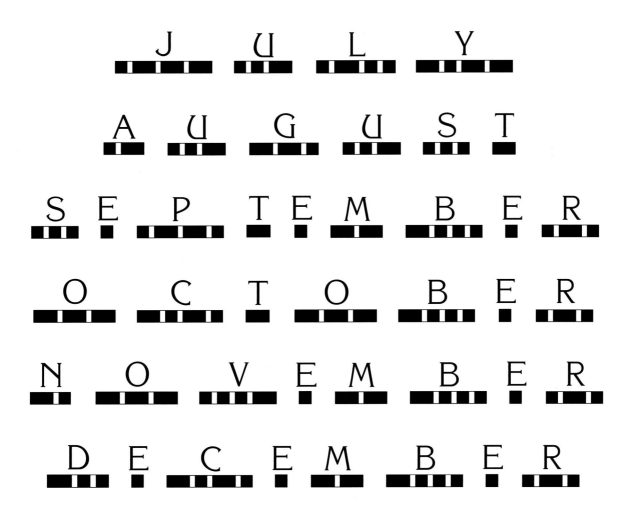

The World Awaits

Quilt

Finished Size:
76" x 86" (193.04 x 218.44cm)

Quilted by Sarabeth Rebe

Graduation is always a time of celebration and new beginnings. This quilt says "The world awaits, MHS, Class of 18" and was a gift to my graduating niece.

Customize this quilt for your own graduate by substituting the graduate's school initials and year, and consider using school colors or the recipient's favorite colors.

The word "world" determined the width of my quilt. Adjust the length by adjusting the width of fabric rows between and on top and bottom of your message rows.

Materials

- ¼ yard (22.86cm) white print, or color of your choice, for letters
- 5½ yards (502.92cm) blue print, or color of your choice, for background and binding
- 5 yards (457.2cm) backing fabric

WOF = width of fabric

General Cutting Instructions

From the white print, cut:

(46) 2½" (6.35cm) A squares

(31) 2½" x 4½" (6.35 x 11.43cm) B rectangles

Note: To avoid seams in the middle of the quilt top, I cut the blue background strips from the length of fabric, or running yardage. Cut the long strips first, then cut the smaller squares and rectangles for spacers from the leftover yardage. Keep your cuts organized by size and color to make quilt assembly easier.

From the blue print, cut:

(6) 6½" x 76½" (16.51 x 194.31cm) strips from running yardage for row spacers

(1) 18½" x 76½" (46.99 x 194.31cm) strip from running yardage for quilt top

(1) 16½" x 76½" (41.91 x 194.31cm) strip from running yardage for quilt bottom

From leftover blue print fabric, cut:

(10) 2½" (6.35cm) x WOF strips.
  From the strips, cut:
  (51) 1½" x 2½" (3.81 x 6.35cm)
  C rectangles for unit spacers

  (19) 2½" x 3½" (6.35 x 8.89cm)
  D rectangles for letter spacers

  (2) 2½" x 27½" (6.35 x 69.85cm)
  E rectangles for row 1 ends

  (2) 2½" x 2½" (6.35 x 6.35cm)
  F rectangles for row 2 ends

(2) 2½" x 9" (6.35 x 22.86cm)
G rectangles for row 3 ends

(2) 2½" x 21" (6.35 x 53.34cm)
H rectangles for row 4 ends

(2) 2½" x 6½" (6.35 x 16.51cm)
I rectangles for row 5 ends

(2) 2½" x 23" (6.35 x 58.42cm)
J rectangles for row 6 ends

(2) 2½" x 15½" (6.35 x 39.37cm)
K rectangles for row 7 ends

(5) 2½" (6.35cm) x WOF binding strips

Piecing the Quilt Top

1. Referring to the illustrations, assemble the seven pieced rows, using accurate ¼" (0.64cm) seams. Press seam allowances toward the blue print. Each row should measure 2½" x 76½" (6.35 x 194.31cm) unfinished.

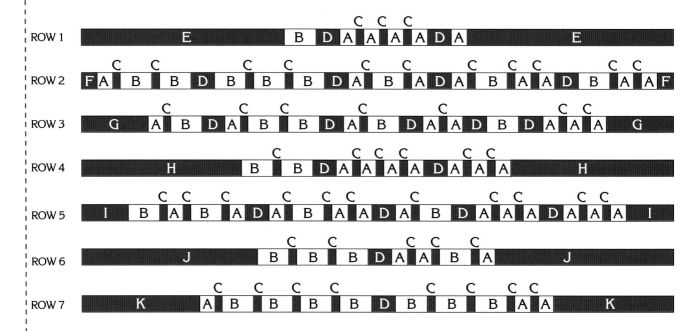

2. Sew the rows together, alternating with the 6½" (16.51cm) background strips. Add an 18½" (46.99cm) background strip to the top of the stitched rows. Add a 16½" (41.91cm) background strip to the bottom of the quilt center.

Finishing the Quilt

1. Layer the quilt top, batting, and backing together. Quilt as desired.

2. Sew the binding strips together, end-to-end, or on the bias, to make one long binding strip. Press seams open.

3. Press the strip, wrong sides together. Sew to the front of the quilt along the raw edges. Fold the binding to the back, covering the raw edges. Hand stitch in place.

Message in the Dark

Quilt

Finished Size:
62½" x 72½" (158.75 x 184.15cm)
Quilted by Sarabeth Rebe

This is the quilt that started my Morse Code journey. As my youngest daughter was preparing to leave for college, hundreds of miles from home, I hoped she would take one of my quilts along to decorate her room. But nothing I had made in the past fit in with her bold, graphical style or bright, saturated color palette. Determined to send along some reminder of home, I designed "Message in the Dark."

The bold solids match her decor, and I'm happy knowing she is protected by my ever-present thought: "To the moon and back, Love, Mom."

Materials
- 4¾ yards (434.34cm) dark blue for background and binding
- ¼ yard (22.86cm) jade green for letters
- ⅜ yard (34.29cm) purple for letters
- ¼ yard (22.86cm) bright turquoise for letters
- ¼ yard (22.86cm) dark teal for letters
- 5 yards (457.2cm) backing fabric

WOF = width of fabric

General Cutting Instructions

Note: To avoid seams in the middle of the quilt top, I cut the background strips from the length of fabric, or running yardage. Cut the long strips first, then cut the smaller squares and rectangles for spacers from the leftover yardage.

Keep your cuts organized by size and color to make quilt assembly easier.

From dark blue background fabric, cut running yardage:
(1) 13½" x 63" (34.29 x 160.02cm) strip for row 1

(6) 5½" x 63" (13.97 x 160.02cm) strips for rows 3, 5, 7, 9, 11, and 13

(1) 15½" x 63" (39.37 x 160.02cm) strip for row 15

From jade green, cut the following for rows 2 and 14:
(2) 2½" (6.35cm) x WOF strips
   From the strips, cut:
   (11) 2½" x 4½" (6.35 x 11.43cm) B rectangles

From purple, cut the following for rows 4, 8, and 12:
(3) 2½" (6.35cm) x WOF strips
   From the strips, cut:
   (9) 2½" x 4½" (6.35 x 11.43cm) B rectangles

   (16) 2½" (6.35cm) A squares

From bright turquoise, cut the following for row 6:
(2) 2½" (6.35cm) x WOF strips
   From the strips, cut:
   (9) 2½" x 4½" (6.35 x 11.43cm) B rectangles

   (1) 2½" (6.35cm) A square

From dark teal, cut the following for row 8:
(2) 2½" (6.35cm) x WOF strips
   From the strips, cut:
   (6) 2½" x 4½" (6.35 x 11.43cm) B rectangles

   (7) 2½" (6.35cm) A squares

From the leftover dark blue background fabric, cut:
(1) 3½" (8.89cm) x WOF strip
   From the strip, cut:
   (16) 2½" x 3½" (6.35 x 8.89cm) D rectangles for rows 2, 4, 6, 8, 10, 12, and 14 for letter spacers

(14) 2½" (6.35cm) x WOF strips
   From the strips, cut:
   (36) 1½ x 2½" (3.81 x 6.35cm) C rectangles for unit spacers

(2) 2½" x 18¼" (6.35 x 46.36cm) E rectangles for row 2 ends

(2) 2½" x 19¾" (6.35 x 50.17cm) F rectangles for row 4 ends

(2) 2½" x 5¾" (6.35 x 14.61cm) G rectangles for row 6 ends

(2) 2½" x 16¼" (6.35 x 41.91cm) H rectangles for row 8 ends

(2) 2½" x 4¼" (6.35 x 10.80cm) I rectangles for row 10 ends

(2) 2½" x 4¼" (6.35 x 10.80cm) J rectangles for row 12 ends

(2) 2½" x 12¼" (6.35 x 31.12cm) K rectangles for row 14 ends

(7) 2½" (6.35cm) x WOF binding strips

Because some rows have more pieces than others, it's important to use an accurate ¼" (0.64cm) seam when sewing the rows.

Piecing the Quilt Top

1. Sew the pieces for rows 2, 4, 6, 8, 10, 12, and 14 together, following the illustrations.

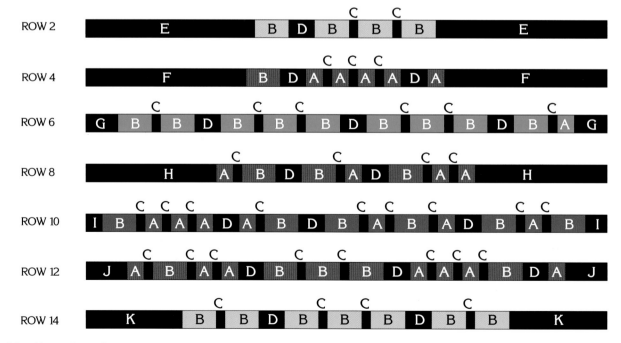

2. Sew 5½" x 63" (13.97 x 160.02cm) dark blue strips between each row.

3. Sew a 13½" x 63" (34.29 x 160.02cm) dark blue strip to the top of the quilt center.

4. Sew a 5½" x 63" (13.97 x 160.02cm) dark blue strip to the bottom of the quilt center.

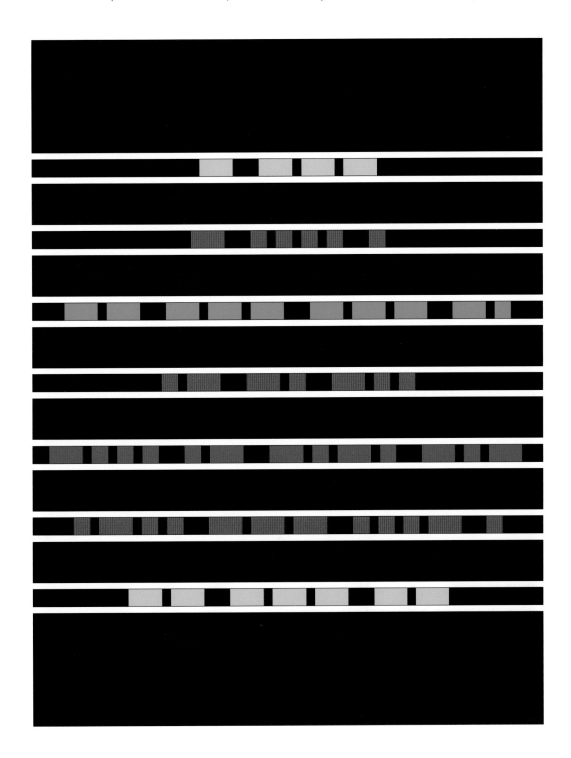

Finishing the Quilt

1. Layer the quilt top, batting, and backing together. Quilt as desired.

2. Sew the binding strips together, end-to-end, or on the bias, to make one long binding strip. Press seams open.

3. Press the strip, wrong sides together. Sew to the front of the quilt along the raw edges. Fold the binding to the back, covering the raw edges. Hand stitch in place.

Love You More

Quilt

Finished Size:
42" x 50" (106.68 x 127cm)
Quilted by Sarabeth Rebe

"Love you more"...
a heartfelt sentiment often said in reply to "I love you." This simple message is easily the focus of this throw-sized quilt. Pick the receiver's favorite color for the background and pick a contrasting solid or tonal print for the letters for maximum impact.

Materials
- ¼ yard (22.86cm) white print for letters
- 3¼ yards (297.18cm) orange fabric for background and binding
- 3 yards (274.32cm) backing fabric

WOF = width of fabric

General Cutting Instructions
From the white print, cut:
(13) 2" (5.08cm) A squares

(18) 2" x 3½" (5.08 x 8.89cm) B rectangles

Note: To avoid seams in the middle of the quilt top, I cut the orange background strips from the length of fabric, or running yardage. Cut the long strips first, then cut the smaller squares and rectangles for spacers from the leftover yardage. Keep your cuts organized by size and color to make quilt assembly easier.

From orange background fabric, cut:
(2) 6½" x 42½" (16.51 x 107.95cm) strips from running yardage for row spacers

(1) 12½" x 42½" (31.75 x 107.95cm) strip from running yardage for top of quilt center

(1) 20½" x 42½" (52.07 x 107.95cm) strip from running yardage for bottom of quilt center

From leftover orange fabric, cut:
(4) 2" (5.08cm) x WOF strips.
From the strips, cut:
(20) 1¼" x 2" (3.18 x 5.08cm) C rectangles for unit spacers

(8) 2¾" x 2" (6.99 x 5.08cm) D rectangles for letter spacers

(2) 1⅞" x 2" (4.76 x 5.08cm) E rectangles for row 1 ends

(2) 3⅜" x 2" (8.57 x 5.08cm) F rectangles for row 2 ends

(2) 4½" x 2"(11.43 x 5.08cm) G rectangles for row 3 ends

(5) 2½" (6.35cm) binding strips

Piecing the Quilt Top

1. Referring to the illustrations, assemble the three letter rows. Press seams toward the background fabric.

Each row should measure 42½" (107.95cm) unfinished.

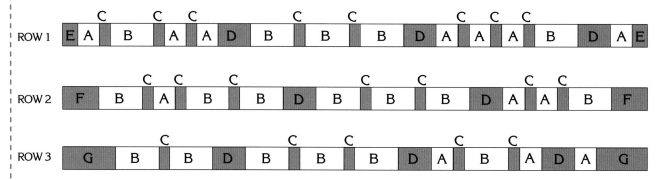

2. Sew the rows together, alternating with the 6½" (16.51cm) orange background strips.

3. Sew a 12½" (31.75cm) background strip to the top of the rows.

4. Sew a 20½" (52.07cm) background strip to the bottom of the rows.

Finishing the Quilt

1. Layer the quilt top, batting, and backing together. Quilt as desired.

2. Sew the binding strips together, end-to-end, or on the bias, to make one long binding strip. Press seams open.

3. Press the strip, wrong sides together. Sew to the front of the quilt along the raw edges. Fold the binding to the back, covering the raw edges. Hand stitch in place.

Love Is Love

Quilt

Finished Size:
27½" x 27½" (69.85 x 69.85cm)

Quilted by Sarabeth Rebe

A message can be
communicated with
the Morse code letters
and with color.

This quilt is a special
message for my sister,
Kathy. Using a rainbow of
colors and the simple words,
"Love is love,"
I'm sending her a
message of encouragement
and affirmation.

Materials
- 1 yard (91.44cm) black solid background and binding fabric
- Scraps for 28 different prints in a rainbow of colors

WOF = width of fabric

General Cutting Instructions
Keep your cuts organized by size and color to make quilt assembly easier.

From assorted scraps, cut:

(19) 1" x 1½" (2.54 x 3.81cm) A rectangles for letter units

(10) 1" x 2½" (2.54 x 6.35cm) B rectangles for letter units

From the black solid fabric, cut:

(2) 5½" x 28" (13.97 x 71.12cm) strips for space between letter rows

(1) 7½" x 28" (19.05 x 71.12cm) strip for top of quilt center

(1) 8½" x 28" (21.59 x 71.12cm) strip for bottom of quilt center

(4) 1" (2.54cm) x WOF strips
   From the strips, cut:
   (19) 1" (2.54cm) C squares for unit spacers

   (7) 1" x 2" (2.54 x 5.08cm) D rectangles for letter spacers

   (4) 1" (2.54 cm) E squares for row 1 and row 3 ends

   (2) 1" x 9¾" (2.54 x 24.77cm) F rectangles for row 2 ends

(2) 2½" (3.65cm) binding strips

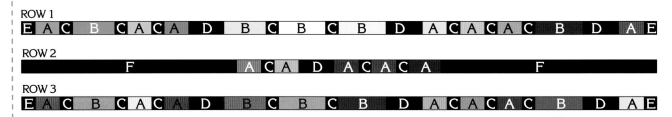

Piecing the Quilt Top

1. Referring to the illustrations, assemble the three pieced rows. Use an accurate ¼" (0.64cm) seam and press seams toward the background fabric. Each row should measure 28" (71.12cm) unfinished.

ROW 1

| E | A | C | B | C | A | C | A | D | B | C | B | C | B | D | A | C | A | C | A | C | B | D | A | E |

ROW 2

| F | A | C | A | D | A | C | A | C | A | F |

ROW 3

| E | A | C | B | C | A | C | A | D | B | C | B | C | B | D | A | C | A | C | A | C | B | D | A | E |

2. Sew the rows together, alternating with the 5½" (13.97cm) background strips.

3. Sew a 7½" (19.05cm) background strip to the top of the rows.

4. Sew an 8½" (21.59cm) strip to the bottom of the rows.

Finishing the Quilt

1. Layer the quilt top, batting, and backing together. Quilt as desired.

2. Sew the binding strips together, end-to-end, or on the bias, to make one long binding strip. Press seams open.

3. Press the strip, wrong sides together. Sew to the front of the quilt along the raw edges. Fold the binding to the back, covering the raw edges. Hand stitch in place.

Peace
Wall Hanging

Finished Size:
48" x 48" (121.92 x 121.92cm)

Quilted by Sarabeth Rebe

The Peace quilt can be a constant reminder to find calm, serenity, or a quiet moment in our daily lives.

Materials

- ⅓ yard (30.45cm) pink print for letters
- 2¼ yards (205.74cm) light blue print for background
- ½ yard (45.72cm) turquoise print binding fabric
- 3 yards (274.32cm) backing fabric

General Cutting Instructions

Keep pieces organized by letter and size for quicker assembly.

From the pink print, cut:

(7) 4½" (11.43cm) A squares

(5) 4½" x 8½" (11.43 x 21.59cm) B rectangles

From the light blue background print, cut:

(4) 4½" (11.43cm) x WOF strips
   From the strips, cut:

   (7) 2½" x 4½" (6.35 x 11.43cm) C rectangles for spacers

   (4) 4½" x 9¼" (11.43 x 23.5cm) D rectangles for row 1 and row 4 ends

   (4) 4½" x 22¼" (11.43 x 56.52cm) E rectangles for row 2 and row 5 ends

   (2) 4½" x 17¼" (11.43 x 43.82cm) F rectangles for row 3 ends

(1) 48½" (123.19cm) x WOF strip
   From running yardage, cut:

   (4) 4½" x 49" (11.43 x 124.46cm) strips for row spacers

   (2) 6½" x 49" (16.51 x 124.46cm) strips for outer vertical sides

From the turquoise print, cut:

(5) 2½" (6.35cm) x WOF strips for binding

Piecing the Quilt Top

Unlike traditional quilts, this top is assembled in vertical rows. It's a nice change from a horizontal look.

1. Referring to the diagrams, assemble the five pieced rows, using an accurate ¼" (0.64cm) seam. The rows should measure 49" (124.46cm) unfinished. Press the seams away from the letter fabric. I like to include specialty quilting in these areas so it makes it easier to stitch.

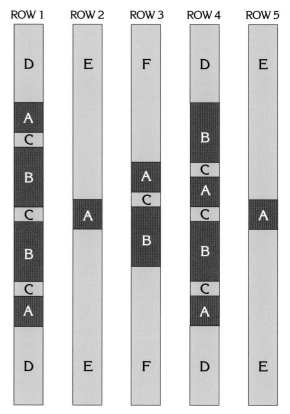

2. Sew the rows together, alternating with the 4¼" x 49" (11.43 x 124.46cm) strips. Sew the 6½" x 49" (16.51 x 124.46cm) strips to either side of the outermost edges of the quilt. Press the rows toward the background fabric.

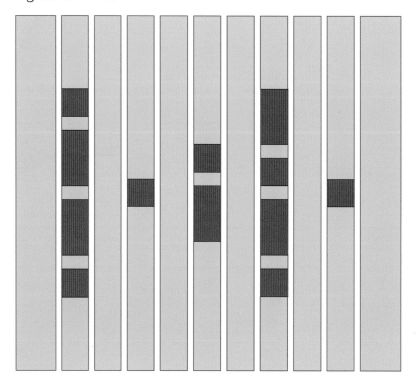

Finishing the Quilt

1. Layer the quilt top, batting, and backing together. Quilt as desired.

2. Sew the binding strips together, end-to-end, or on the bias, to make one long binding strip. Press seams open.

3. Press the strip, wrong sides together. Sew to the front of the quilt along the raw edges. Fold the binding to the back, covering the raw edges. Hand stitch in place.

Merry

Wall Hanging

Finished Size:
25½" x 25½" (64.77 x 64.77cm)

Quilted by Sarabeth Rebe

The holidays are a perfect time for modern takes on seasonal decor.

This wall hanging can be left out all winter long.
Each row depicts one letter in the word "Merry."

Materials

- ¼ yard (22.86cm) red solid for letters
- 1¼ yard (114.3cm) gray print background and binding fabric
- 1 yard (91.44cm) backing fabric

WOF = width of fabric

General Cutting Instructions

Keep your cuts organized by size and color to make quilt assembly easier.

From the red print, cut:

(6) 2½" (6.35cm) A squares

(7) 2½" x 4½" (6.35 x 11.43cm) B rectangles

From the gray print, cut:

(4) 2½" (6.35cm) x WOF strips
    From the strips, cut:
    (8) 2½" x 1½" (6.35 x 3.81cm) C rectangles for spacers

    (2) 2½" x 8¼" (6.35 x 20.96cm) D rectangles for row 1 ends

    (2) 2½" x 11¾" (6.35 x 29.85cm) E rectangles for row 2 ends

    (4) 2½" x 7¾" (6.35 x 19.68cm) F rectangles for row 3 and row 4 ends

    (2) 2½" x 4¼" (6.35 x 10.80cm) G rectangles for row 5 ends

    (4) 2½" x 26" (6.35 x 66.04cm) strips for row spacers

    (2) 3½" x 26" (8.89 x 66.04cm) strips for the top and bottom of the quilt

(3) 2½" (6.35cm) x WOF strips for the binding

Piecing the Quilt Top

1. Referring to the diagrams, assemble the five pieced rows. Use an accurate ¼" (0.64cm) seam. Press the seam allowances toward the background fabric. I like to include specialty quilting or stitches in the word blocks, so I always try to press seams away from these blocks to make stitching easier.

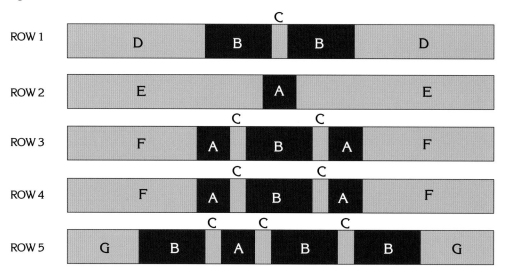

Each row should measure 26" (66.04cm) unfinished.

2. Sew the rows together, alternating with the 2½" x 26" (6.35 x 66.04cm) strips. Sew the 3½" x 26" (8.89 x 66.04cm) strips to the top and bottom of the quilt. Press the rows toward the background fabric.

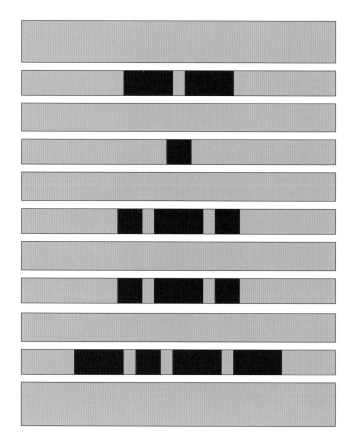

Finishing the Quilt

1. Layer the quilt top, batting, and backing together. Quilt as desired.

2. Sew the binding strips together, end-to-end, or on the bias, to make one long binding strip. Press seams open.

3. Press the strip, wrong sides together. Sew to the front of the quilt along the raw edges. Fold the binding to the back, covering the raw edges. Hand stitch in place.

Hugs
Wall Hanging

Finished Size:
31" x 31" (78.74 x 78.74cm)

Quilted by Sarabeth Rebe

Sometimes you need a
quick way to send
encouragement to a friend.
The "Hugs" wall hanging can
be completed in a day and is
the perfect, subtle message
of support and concern.

Materials
- ⅛ yard (11.43cm) rose-purple print
- ⅛ yard (11.43cm) dusty purple print
- 1 yard (91.44cm) multi-print
  for background
- ⅓ yard (30.45cm) violet print for binding
- 1 yard (30.45cm) backing fabric

WOF = width of fabric

General Cutting Instructions
Keep your cuts organized by size and color to
make quilt assembly easier.

From the rose-purple print, cut:
(5) 3½" (8.89cm) A squares

(2) 3½" x 6½" (8.89 x 16.51cm) B rectangles

From dusty purple print, cut:
(5) 3½" (8.89cm) A squares

(1) 3½" x 6½" (8.89 x 16.51cm) B rectangle

From multi-print, cut:
(3) 3½" (8.89cm) x WOF strips
  From the strips, cut:
  (9) 2" x 3½ (5.08 x 8.89cm) C rectangles for
  unit spacers

  (2) 3½" x 7¼" (8.89 x 18.42cm)
  D rectangles for row 1 ends

  (2) 3½" x 8" (8.89 x 20.32cm) E rectangles
  for row 2 ends

  (2) 3½" x 6½" (8.89 x 16.51cm) F rectangles
  for row 3 ends

  (2) 3½" x 9½" (8.89 x 24.13cm) G
  rectangles for row 4 ends

(2) 4½" x 31½" (11.43 x 80.01cm) strips for
  top and bottom of quilt

(4) 3½" x 31½" (8.89 x 80.01cm) strips for
  space between rows of letters

(4) 2½" (6.35cm) x WOF strips for binding

Piecing the Quilt Top

1. Referring to the diagrams, assemble the four pieced rows. Use an accurate ¼" (0.64cm) seam. Press the seam allowances toward the background fabric. I like to include specialty quilting or stitches in the word blocks, so I always try to press seams away from these blocks to make stitching easier.

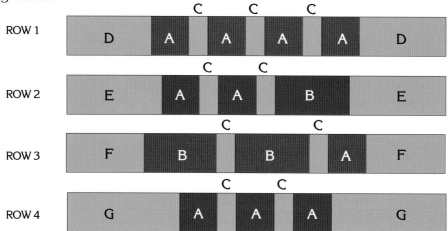

Each row should measure 2½" x 31½" (6.35 x 80.01cm) unfinished.

2. Sew the rows together, alternating with the 3½" x 31½" (8.89 x 80.01cm) strips. Sew the 4½" x 31½" (11.43 x 80.01cm) strips to the top and bottom of the quilt. Press the rows toward the background fabric.

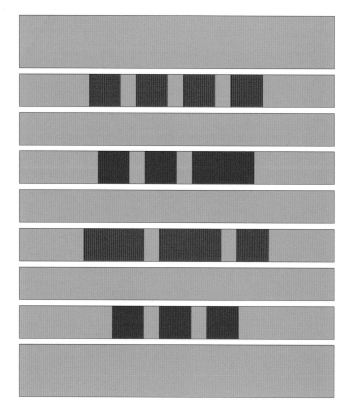

Finishing the Quilt

1. Layer the quilt top, batting, and backing together. Quilt as desired.

2. Sew the binding strips together, end-to-end, or on the bias, to make one long binding strip. Press seams open.

3. Press the strip, wrong sides together. Sew to the front of the quilt along the raw edges. Fold the binding to the back, covering the raw edges. Hand stitch in place.

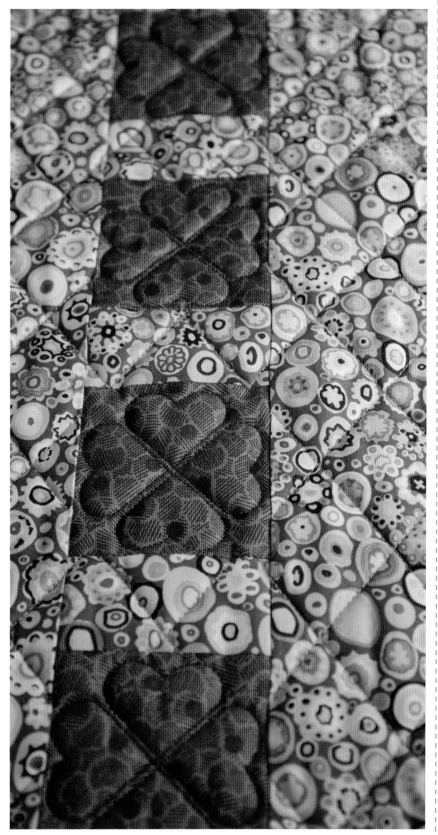

Snow
Wall Hanging

Finished Size:
19" x 31" (48.26 x 78.74cm)

Quilted by Sarabeth Rebe

This seasonal wall hanging or table runner can stay out all winter long with it's simple message welcoming "Snow."

Materials
- ⅛ yard (11.43cm) red print for letters
- ½ yard (45.72cm) multi-print for background
- ⅓ yard (30.45cm) red print for binding
- ¾ yard (68.58cm) backing fabric

WOF = width of fabric

General Cutting Instructions
From the red print for letters, cut:
(5) 2½" (6.35cm) A squares

(6) 2½" x 4½" (6.35 x 11.43cm) B rectangles

From multi-print background fabric, cut:
(3) 2½" (6.35cm) x WOF strips
From the strips, cut:
(7) 1½" x 2½" (3.81 x 6.35cm) C rectangles for unit spacers

(2) 2½" x 11" (6.35 x 27.94cm) D strips for row 1 ends

(2) 2½" x 12" (6.35 x 30.48cm) E strips for row 2 ends

(2) 2½" x 8½" (6.35 x 21.59cm) F strips for row 3 ends

(2) 2½" x 9½" (6.35 x 24.13cm) G strips for row 4 ends

(5) 2½" x 31½" (6.35 x 80.01cm) strips for top and bottom of quilt center, row spacers

From the red binding fabric, cut:
(3) 2½" (6.35cm) x WOF strips for binding

Piecing the Quilt Top

1. Referring to the diagrams, assemble the four pieced rows. Use an accurate ¼" (0.64cm) seam. Press the seam allowances toward the background fabric. I like to include specialty quilting or stitches in the word blocks, so I always try to press seams away from these blocks to make stitching easier.

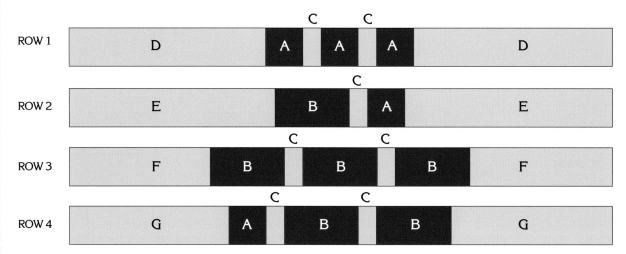

The rows should measure 31½" (80.01cm) unfinished.

2. Sew the rows together, alternating with the 2½" x 31½" (6.35 x 80.01cm) strips. Sew the 2½" x 31½" (6.35 x 80.01cm) strips to the top and bottom of the quilt. Press the rows towards the background fabric.

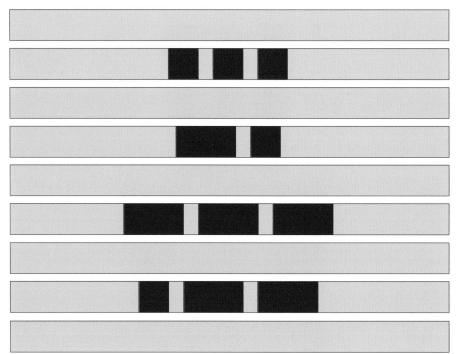

Finishing the Quilt

1. Layer the quilt top, batting, and backing together. Quilt as desired.

2. Sew the binding strips together, end-to-end, or on the bias, to make one long binding strip. Press seams open.

3. Press the strip, wrong sides together. Sew to the front of the quilt along the raw edges. Fold the binding to the back, covering the raw edges. Hand stitch in place.

Across the Myles

Throw

Finished Size:
41" x 55" (104.14 x 139.7cm)

Quilted by Sarabeth Rebe

Using Morse code to spell out a special someone's name is a quick and easy way to create a special gift. My niece, Myles, loves yellow and pink, so I settled on this combination to make a quilt she can use at nap time.

When creating a name for your quilt, the longest letter will determine the width of your quilt. In my quilt, the letter "Y" took up the most space. I wanted a smaller-sized throw, so I needed to adjust the size of the units in the letters. If the name has several letters, consider decreasing the width of the background strips in between the letters so your quilt doesn't become too long in relation to the width.

To make your quilt, start by writing out the name you want to use and calculate how many units for each letter, using the chart on pages 10–11. From there, assign a size to dots, dashes, and spacers to fit your quilt. See page 8.

Materials

The yardage is given to make a 41" x 55" (104.14 x 139.7cm) finished quilt. Since you will be creating a quilt with your chosen name, the fabric for letters may or may not be enough. To start calculating your letters, you could use my predetermined height of dots, dashes, and spacers, which is 2½" (6.35cm).

- ¼ yard (22.86cm) yellow print for letters
- 2¼ yards (205.74cm) bright pink for background and binding
- 2⅞ yard (262.89cm) backing fabric

WOF = width of fabric

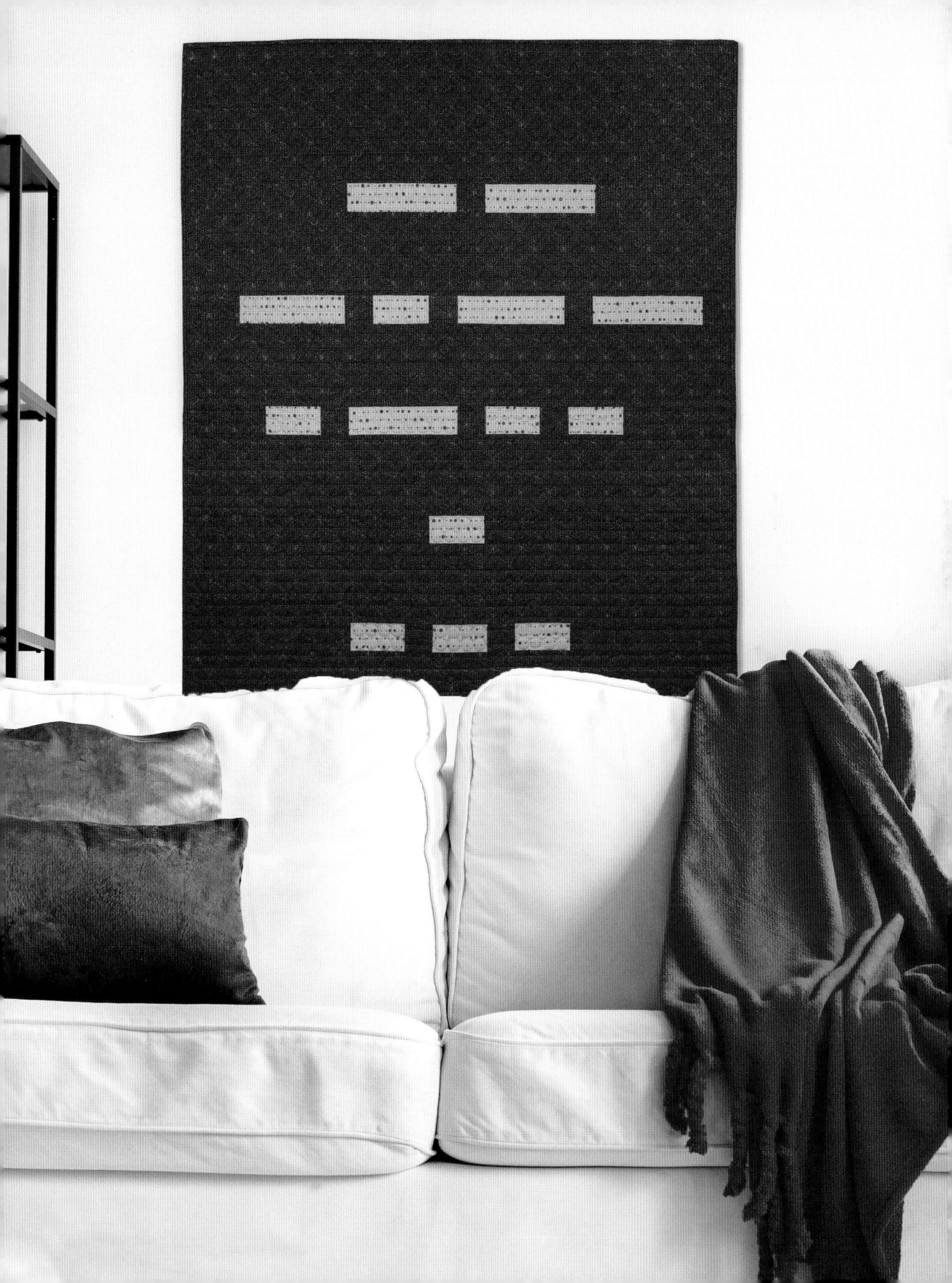

General Cutting Instructions

1. When you have determined the size and number of dots, dashes, and spacers you need, cut units, including a ½" (3.81cm) unit, and keep them organized by size and color to make quilt assembly easier. Dots and dashes will be cut from your chosen fabric for letters. Spacers will be your chosen background fabric.

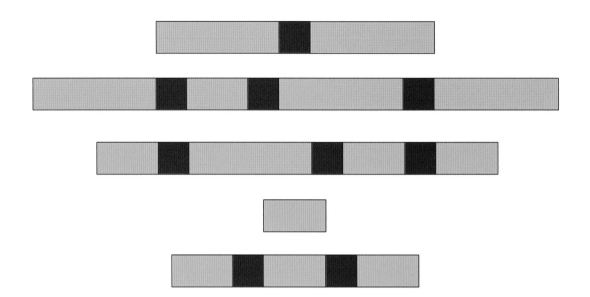

2. Sew the letter rows together.

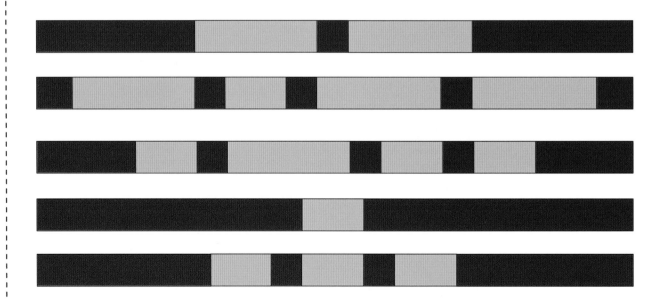

3. Sew strips of background fabric to the ends of the letter rows to equal the width of your unfinished quilt. You can either center the letter rows on the quilt center, or stagger them side to side for a more modern, free-form look.

4. To cut strips for row spacers, determine the height of the strips and cut to the width of your unfinished quilt. Remember to keep these strips a reasonable height so the length of your quilt doesn't become too long in relation to the width of your quilt.

5. Sew the strips from step 4 in between the letter rows.

6. Add fabric strips to the top and the bottom of the quilt center to finish the quilt.

7. Measure the sides, and top and bottom of the quilt to determine the length of binding fabric. Cut strips 2½" (6.35cm) wide.

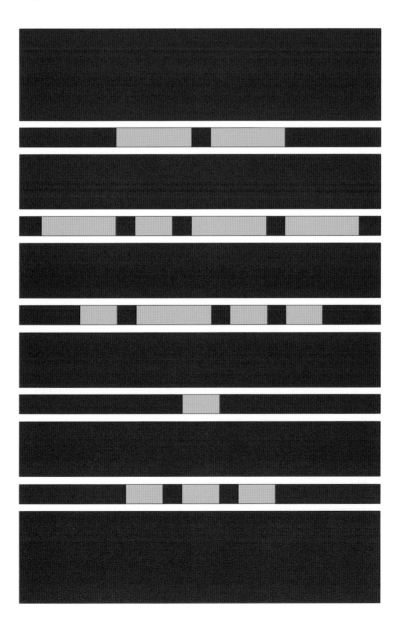

Finishing the Quilt

1. Layer the quilt top, batting, and backing together. Quilt as desired.

2. Sew the binding strips together, end-to-end, or on the bias, to make one long binding strip. Press seams open.

3. Press the strip, wrong sides together. Sew to the front of the quilt along the raw edges. Fold the binding to the back, covering the raw edges. Hand stitch in place.

The Adventure Begins

Quilt

Finished Size:
98" x 106" (248.92 x 269.24cm)

Quilted by Sarabeth Rebe

When my daughter announced her engagement, I knew I wanted to make her a quilt to celebrate her wedding day. The quilt says "And so the adventure begins, Megan and Tyler, October 14, 2017.".

Customize the quilt for your own special event by replacing names and dates for rows 6–11. Materials list is for a king-size quilt. The first five lines of the quilt will work with any quilt, so cutting and sewing instructions are only given for the words, "and so the adventure begins".

You will need to calculate your message for names and dates. Refer to pages 7–8. I've listed the measurements for dots, dashes, and spacers, reflecting those used for the general message. Use these calculations to apply to your message for size consistency.

The following measurements are unfinished:
- Dots: 2½" (6.35cm) squares
- Dashes: 2½" x 4½" (6.35 x 11.43cm)
- Unit spacers: 1½" x 2½" (3.81 x 6.35cm)
- Letter spacers: 2½" x 3½" (6.35 x 8.89cm)
- Rows between letters are 2½" x 98½" (6.35 x 250.19cm) unfinished

Materials
- 1 yard (91.44cm) dark blue print for letters
- 11 yards (1005.84cm) blue-gray print for background and binding
- 9 yards (822.96cm) backing fabric

WOF = width of fabric

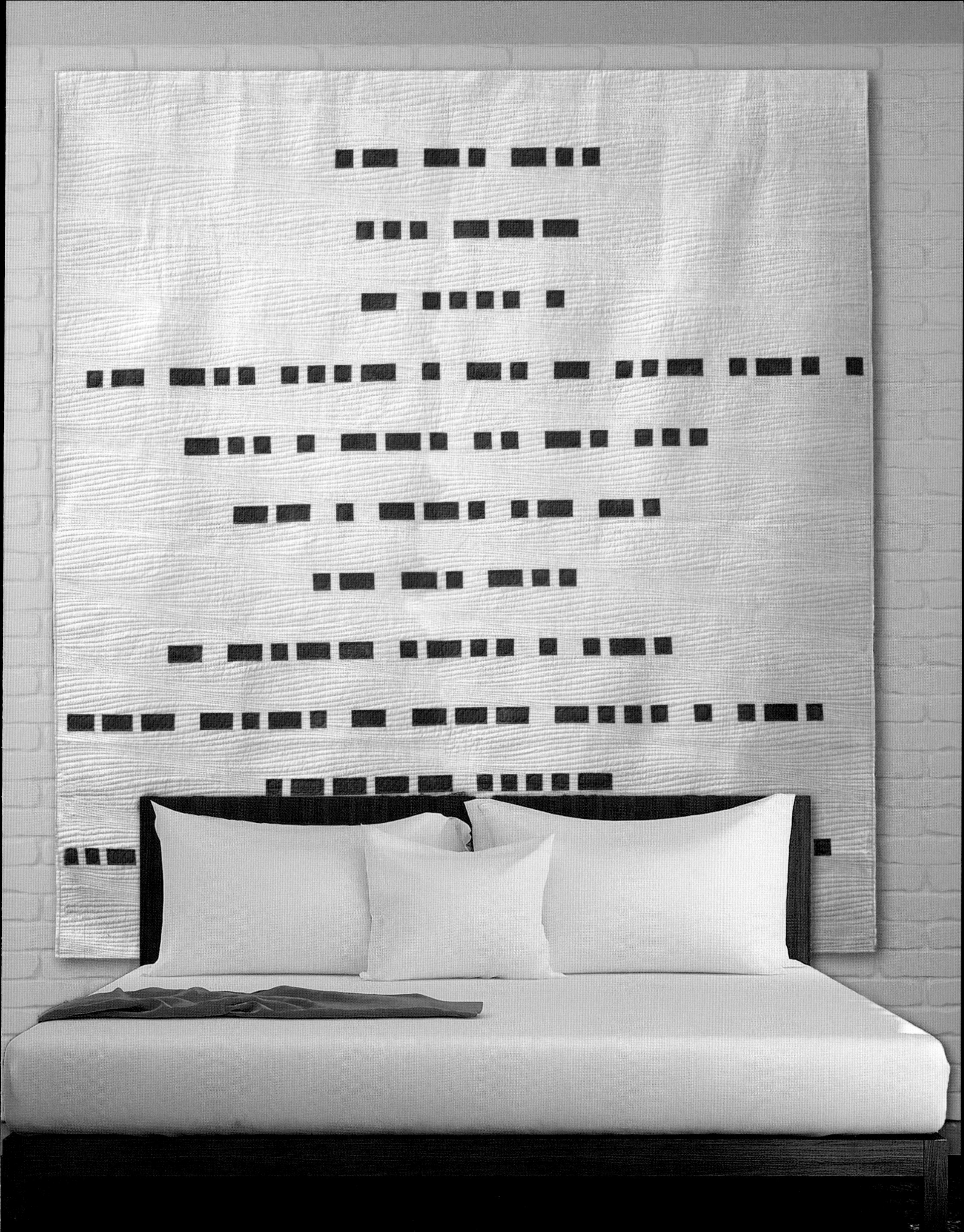

General Cutting Instructions

From the dark blue print, cut:

(35) 2½" (6.35cm) A squares for letters

(18) 2½" x 4½" (6.35 x 11.43cm) B rectangles for letters

Note: To avoid seams in the middle of the quilt top, I cut the blue-gray background strips from the length of fabric, or running yardage. Cut the long strips first, then cut the smaller squares and rectangles for spacers from the leftover yardage. Keep your cuts organized by size and color to make quilt assembly easier.

From the blue-gray print, cut:

(4) 6½" x 98½" (16.51 x 250.19cm) strips from running yardage

(1) 10½" x 98½" (26.67 x 250.19cm) strip from running yardage

(1) 12½" x 98½" (31.75 x 250.19cm) strip from running yardage

From leftover fabric, cut:

(24) 2½" (6.35cm) x WOF strips
From the strips, cut:
(30) 1½" x 2½" (3.81 x 6.35cm) C rectangles for unit spacers

(18) 2½" x 3½" (6.35 x 8.89cm) D rectangles for letter spacers

(2) 2½" x 34" (6.35 x 86.36cm) E rectangles for row 1 ends

(2) 2½" x 36½" (6.35 x 92.71cm) F rectangles for row 2 ends

(2) 2½" x 37½" (6.35 x 95.25cm) G rectangles for row 3 ends

(2) 2½" x 4½" (6.35 x 11.43cm) H rectangles for row 4 ends

(2) 2½" x 18½" (6.35 x 46.99cm) I rectangles for row 5 ends

(9) 2½" (6.35cm) strips for the binding if your unfinished quilt measures 98½" x 106½" (250.19 x 270.51cm)

Piecing the Quilt Top

1. Since the names and dates will differ on your own quilt, refer to the illustrations and assemble the first five rows of the quilt to complete "and so the adventure begins." Replace your information in the last six rows. Assemble the rows, using an accurate ¼" (0.64cm) seam. Press seam allowances toward the gray background fabric.

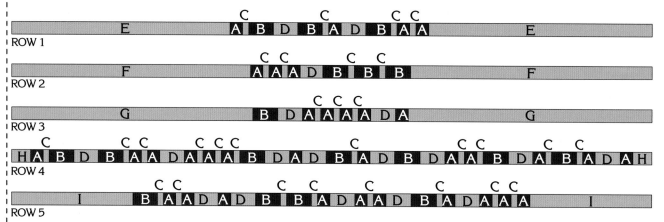

Each row should measure 98½" (250.19cm) unfinished

2. Sew the rows together, alternating with the 6½" (16.51cm) background strips. Continue using 6½" (16.51cm) strips between the rows of your own text. When the message part of your quilt is complete, add spacers to the top and bottom of the message

Finishing the Quilt

1. Layer the quilt top, batting, and backing together. Quilt as desired.

2. Sew the binding strips together, end-to-end, or on the bias, to make one long binding strip. Press seams open.

3. Press the strip, wrong sides together. Sew to the front of the quilt along the raw edges. Fold the binding to the back, covering the raw edges. Hand stitch in place.

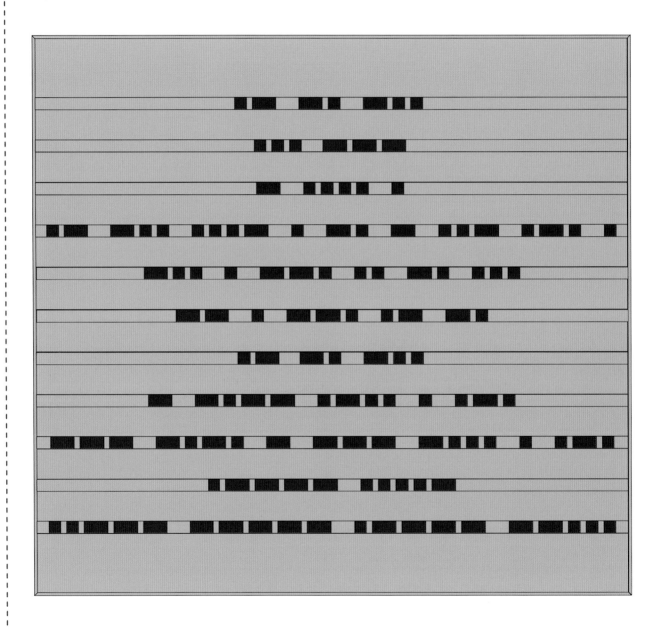

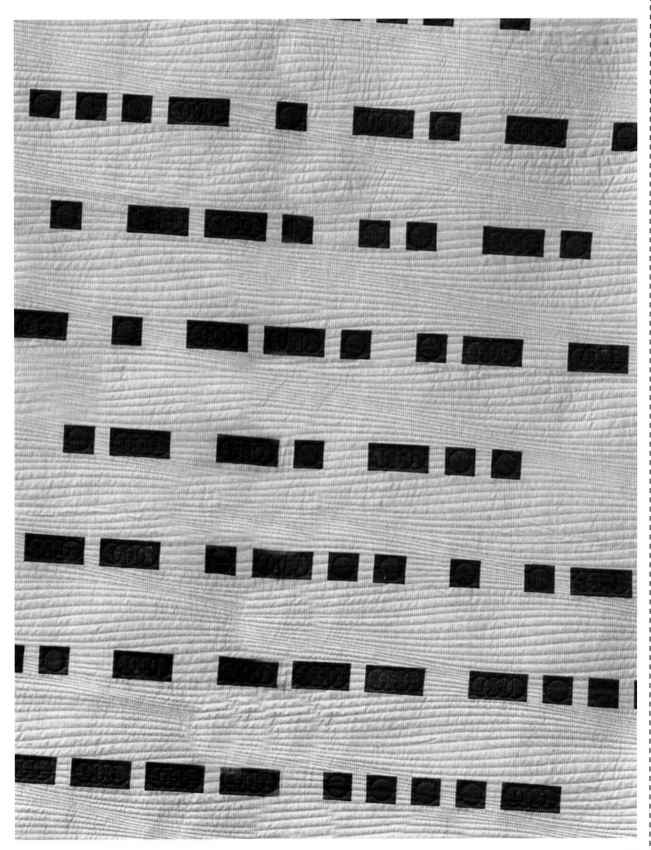

About the Author

Sarah's love of quilting stems from her college days, when her mom sent her a pink dogwood quilt to grace the bed in her first apartment. The quilt was a comforting reminder of her home in the Lake of the Ozarks, where the dogwood blossoms always signaled the start of spring.

A few years later, married and expecting her first child, Sarah caught the nesting bug. Inspired by the treasured dogwood quilt, she bought a *Teach Yourself to Quilt* book and crafted her first quilt. She continued to improve her skills through classes at local quilt guilds, as well as learning from gifted teachers throughout the United States, fully taking advantage of modern conveniences, such as rotary cutting and computer design, as they became available.

Today, Sarah is a fabric and pattern designer for Studio 37 Fabrics, a division of Marcus Fabrics, with countless quilts to her credit. Her work has been featured regularly in both *McCall's Quilting* and *McCall's Quick Quilts* for the past several years. Additionally, Sarah's quilts have appeared in *Make Modern, Simply Moderne, American Patchwork & Quilting*, and *Quilts & More*, as well as many other magazines.